Look - Book 1
VI

By Viola & Zaida Stefano

The rights of Viola & Zaida Stefano to be identified as the authors of this work have been asserted by them in accordance with the **Copyright Amendment (Moral Rights) Act 2000.**

All rights reserved. Apart from any use as permitted by the authors & under the **Copyright Act 1968**, no part may be reproduced, copied, scanned, stored in a retrieval system, recorded, or shared, by any means or in any form, without prior written permission from the publisher.

A catalogue record of this book is available from the **National Library of Australia.**

ISBN: 978-0-6456272-4-4

Authors: Viola Stefano & Zaida Stefano
Illustrations, cover & internal designs: Zaida Stefano

Illustrations copyright © Zaida Stefano 2023
Design copyright © Zaida Stefano 2023

Disclaimer: The content presented in this book is meant for educational purposes only. The authors & publisher claim no accountability to any entity or person for any liability, damage, or loss caused or assumed to be caused directly or indirectly as a consequence of the application, use, or interpretation of the material in this book.

VeeZee Publications

Copyright © VeeZee Publications Pty Ltd 2023
First published in Australia in 2023
by VeeZee Publications Pty Ltd
veezeepublications.com

Learning made easy with

VeeZee!

- Focus Core words in 'Look - Book 1' and the 'Look' series
- Secondary Core words in 'Look - Book 1' and the 'Look' series
- Other secondary Core words in the 'Look' series but **NOT** in 'Look - Book 1'

Core Vocabulary used throughout **VeeZee Publications**				
I	**want**	**can**	stop	**look**
like	**more**	he	go	**see**
here	what	**do**	**the**	**and**
out	where	**we**	**it**	**up**
not	they	when	**that**	**down**
she	**now**	**them**	is	put
help	off	**you**	**yes**	on
turn	who	**this**	**no**	why
done	make	**a**	**to**	**under**
come	in	**some**	which	**there**
open	get	good	same	home

Supporting students with low vision (vision impairment - VI)

Our VI range has been especially developed to give children with low vision the very best opportunity to learn. The illustrations in the VI version of the readers, replicate key elements of the photographs included in the other version of the readers. We have done this so that all students engage with the same content. Yellow framing is used around each illustration to support children with low vision to focus on the illustrations more readily. Each book is carefully designed with deliberate and strategic use of colour, background and contrast for typescript and for illustrations. Placing these colours onto a black background supports children with low vision to see the illustrations more successfully because of the contrast provided. Teachers should provide guidance to their students by talking about the colours, lines and themes of each illustration. Ask questions using Core words; who, what, where, when and why, to reinforce their associations with surrounding words. The illustrations with their vibrant colours included in our VI range have been created to promote student interest, engagement and learning. Please ensure that classroom lighting provides optimal conditions for students to engage with the VI readers. We advise that students without a vision impairment also explore the readers designed for students with low vision. This will support interaction and discussion amongst the students. It is our hope that this will ultimately promote acceptance, understanding, compassion and teamwork, thus cultivating true inclusion.

We hope you have fun discovering what animals are in our 'Look' books. Not all of our animals have been named, so good luck with your research!

Book 1 Key Colours

Where do tigers live?

Look.

2

Look here.

Look there.

Look now.

Look here now.

Look there now.

Come look mum.

Come look dad.

Come look here mum and dad.

Look there mum and dad.

Look at them.

Look at them now.

Look at them now, mum and dad.

We can look at them here.

We can look at them there.

Look at them here, and look at them there.

Words in this book

here	at	come
there	look	mum

Words in this book

them	now	and
we	dad	can

Do you know the focus and secondary Core words: 'look', 'here' and 'now'? Read the words along each line.

look	look	here	now	look	now	look
here	look	look	now	here	look	now
now	look	now	look	look	here	now
now	look	look	now	here	look	now
look	here	now	look	look	here	look
here	look	here	now	look	look	now
look	now	here	look	here	now	look

Do you know the focus and secondary Core words in this book (refer to Core word table)? Find them along each line, point to them and say them. Read the other words too once you have pointed to the Core words.

look	here	mum	there	look	now	can
at	and	there	now	mum	here	come
there	look	now	look	here	we	dad
now	mum	here	and	them	at	look
here	dad	now	mum	look	come	there
dad	come	look	here	we	mum	now
mum	now	there	can	now	look	here

How many times did you read the word 'look'?

Make new words with '___ow', e.g., 'slow'. Write sentences using these words.

We hope you had fun reading!

VeeZee Publications

Wait, there's more!

Visit our website for information about our range of readers & supporting products.

veezeepublications.com

www.ingramcontent.com/pod-product-compliance
Lightning Source LLC
Chambersburg PA
CBHW050853010526
44107CB00047BA/1591